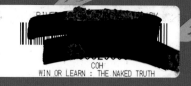

WIN
OR
LEARN

The **Naked Truth** about
Turning Every Rejection into
Your **Ultimate Success**

HARLAN COHEN

Internal images © endsheets, Elena Sazanova/Getty Images; page vi, Andrew Merry/Getty Images; page ix, d3sign/Getty Images; page xii, Westend61/Getty Images; pages 9, 48, 65, 98, Klaus Vedfelt/Getty Images; page 17, Vladimir Vladimirov/Getty Images; page 34, Yellow Dog Productions/Getty Images; page 43, Tom Werner/Getty Images; page 58, Sarah Waiswa/Getty Images; page 69, Hill Street Studios/Getty Images; pages 72, 97, skynesher/Getty Images; page 75, guppys/Getty Images; page 78, Maskot/Getty Images; page 84, digitalskillet/Getty Images; page 93, filadendron/Getty Images; page 114, FG Trade/Getty Images
Internal images on pages 20, 29, 52, 55, 90, 100, and 112 have been provided by Unsplash; these images are licensed under CC0 Creative Commons and have been released by the author for use.

Published by Simple Truths, an imprint of Sourcebooks
P.O. Box 4410, Naperville, Illinois 60567-4410
(630) 961-3900
sourcebooks.com

Printed and bound in China.
OGP 10 9 8 7 6 5 4 3 2 1

To Eva Kaye, Harrison, and Asher:

We are *always* in your corner.

Table of Contents

Introduction

My flight was booked for 10:30 p.m. I arrived at Charlotte Douglas International Airport at 8:15 and noticed the earlier flight was delayed until 9:00. I ran to the gate, arriving there at 8:30. I asked the agent if I could have a seat on the plane.

"No. It's closed."

I politely asked, "Why haven't they closed the doors?"

She explained, "There's an international flight that just landed, and fifty people are on their way. They'll be here any minute."

"If one of them doesn't make it, is there any chance I can have their seat?"

"No, they're all coming."

"Right, but if one doesn't make it—you never know—can I have the seat"?

"They will *all* be there."

"Can I just stand here, and if one doesn't make it, can I have the seat?"

"I can't add you to the list. It's too late."

"I understand, but could you make an exception? I'd love to see my kids before bedtime." I smiled.

I stopped talking. I knew I had reached *that* point. I was going to be okay with whatever happened next. I surrendered to the universe.

A few seconds passed. She raised her head. She looked me in the eyes.

With a half-smile, she said, "What do you do for a living? Are you a lawyer?"

I replied, "No. I'm an expert on rejection."

She burst out laughing. I started laughing too. The woman standing in line listening behind me joined in the laughter.

The agent and I chatted for about ten minutes. I explained that I help people go after what they want, most of the time without being annoying. She said, "Oh, well, you've been annoying." We laughed again.

Fast-forward thirty minutes, and I'm on the plane, sitting in a window seat with an empty seat next to me. Twenty people never made it to the plane due to a computer glitch in U.S. Customs. I got home in time for bedtime.

That time, I got what I wanted. Sometimes, I don't.

Success wasn't about getting a seat on the plane. It was about committing to a process. I didn't require the universe to respond one way or another. I offered what I wanted without conditions. It was a risk-free risk. I would either win or learn. There was no failing. Rejection, shame, and fear weren't options. I was free.

The process you will learn in this book will make life profoundly better and more fulfilling. You will learn how to give yourself permission to dream big. You will no longer fear failure and rejection. You will become an expert at filtering through life's uncomfortable truths. You will tell your story as if it has already happened and love yourself along the way no matter what happens. You will trust and believe that no matter what happens, you will be okay. Adversity, change, and challenges will fuel your curiosity. Rejection will teach you, inform you, and help you get wherever you want to go (or someplace even better). You will be guaranteed success, because success isn't measured by the outcome. It's measured by committing to a process. In the words of Nelson Mandela, "I never lose. I either win or learn."

The best part? Life will become even more interesting. And really, shouldn't life be interesting?

1.

What Do You Want?

> **Without dreams and goals, there is no living, only merely existing, and that is not why we are here.**
> **—MARK TWAIN**

Want Something

I've spent most of my early life not feeling smart enough, attractive enough, skinny enough, successful enough, or good enough. I can be extremely funny at times. I know how to make people laugh and feel good. Humor has been my armor to cover up the pain underneath the surface. At times, I've struggled with insecurity, social anxiety, jealousy, and change. I don't like it when people feel pain. I know how that feels.

I was a fat teenager. I absolutely hate the word *fat*, but that's what people called me. I cried when I had to run the mile in middle school. I had to work incredibly hard to be included. I never had a big group of close friends.

Whenever I faced rejection, I'd make people laugh. It made it seem like I didn't care. But inside, I was hurting. I'd eat to cover up the pain. Food was my addiction. It was legal, and there was plenty. Friday nights in high school included a sixteen-ounce bag of Doritos, a can of nacho cheese sauce, a jar of jalapeno peppers, and a one-pound bag of M&M's, eating as much as I could. Freshman year in high school, I was 192 pounds and five feet not a lot of inches tall. I remember lying on the ground trying to zip my pants. They were crazy tight. My brother's friend asked him if I had to jump from a building to get into my pants. I pretended not to hear him.

What's crazy about it all is that I have a loving, supportive family. My parents have been married for more than fifty years. I had and have so much love around me. I just didn't have it inside me. I know if you're someone who is a survivor of abuse, a recovering addict, a foster child, an orphan, a minority, an immigrant, sick, immobile, impaired, or physically limited, your eyes might roll as you think, "Big deal. He was fat. If only he knew *real* problems." I agree. My problems may have been small, may still be small. But to me, they felt so big. I knew I had so many advantages, yet I was so terribly flawed, so unhappy. This made me feel even more defective and fueled my shame. I didn't want to feel this way. I hated it. And I've dedicated my life to changing it.

This book is a life manual—for anyone at any stage of life who struggles with the sting of rejection and fears taking risks to seek happiness. The process is something you'll need to practice every day. This isn't an overnight fix. It's a shift in mindset. It's forming new habits. Over time, you will get comfortable with the uncomfortable. You'll be free to say what you think and express how you feel. With each risk you take, you will appreciate that you are worthy and capable, no matter the results. This is the formula I've used to transform my body, write bestselling books, train educators, empower leaders, build multiple businesses, find love, get married, stay married, navigate parenting, and eliminate the shame that used to take up too much of my time and energy. Shame is boring. You don't need it anymore.

So what exactly is it that *you* want? What could we change together if you were able to break free of the fear of rejection? What goal is unrealized? What risk are you not taking?

WARNING: WANTING IS DANGEROUS (IF YOU DO IT RIGHT).

A college counselor told Michelle Obama she wasn't "Princeton material," but she applied to the Ivy League school anyway and got in.

What do you *really* want?

A new job? A healthier body? An education? Respect? Love? Self-worth? Friendship? Financial security? We love it when we get what we want. We hate it when we don't. The more emotion you invest in wanting something, the more dangerous it becomes to go after it. You might not get it at first. You can expect to experience rejection along the way.

Rejection is painful. Your brain processes rejection the same way it processes physical pain. When you emotionally invest in wanting something and don't get what you want, your body reacts as if you've been punched in the gut. It hurts, because that's how we are hardwired. You're not weak. You just need to get great at wanting and handling whatever comes next. Like building a callus, you need to build the emotional tolerance to handle the unavoidable discomfort that comes with going after what you want.

Love is the perfect example. It's deeply personal and intensely emotional; most people get hurt during the process. It can be hard to find love, harder to keep love, and even harder to get over it once it's gone. We are experts at hating it and hiding from it. Kids can't even admit it when they have a crush. Adults can be just as reluctant to share their feelings. Here's a common scene that plays out at events when I talk about love:

ME: By a show of hands, how many of you are single?

AUDIENCE: [*Hands go up.*]

ME: By a show of hands, how many of you want some love in your life?

AUDIENCE: [*Half the hands go down.*]

ME: [*I pick someone who put their hand down.*] So you don't want love in your life? You are not interested in love?

AUDIENCE MEMBER: No.

ME: Why not?

AUDIENCE MEMBER: I'm too busy. I have no time.

ME: Okay. I get it. But if someone perfect for you, the total package, approached you and asked you to grab coffee, get a drink, or study together, would you say "No, I'm too busy," or would you say "Yes, I can make some time"?

AUDIENCE MEMBER: [*After some laughter*] I'd say yes! I'd find the time!

ME: So let me get this straight. You *do* want love in your life, but you just do *not* want to do the work to get it. You'll take it if it lands in your lap, but you won't take the risk if there is a chance of getting hurt. True?

AUDIENCE MEMBER: Yes. I guess that's true.

The more you emotionally invest in wanting something, the more vulnerable you allow yourself to be. The more vulnerable you allow yourself to be, the more dangerous it will feel to take the next step and go after what you want.

The Want Muscle

For this process to work for you, you must give yourself permission to want. You need to trust that you will be okay no matter what. Even if you've been hurt, disappointed, or devastated in the past, you need to be willing to open up again and take a risk. Wanting is a muscle. The more you practice using it, the stronger your *want* muscle will become. **When you stop wanting, the muscle weakens.** It's like atrophy, but it's called *wantrophy*. It's an epidemic. Millions of people suffer from it. You might be one of them.

I was recently in a room filled with seventh graders in a rural school. I asked the class, "By a show of hands, how many of you are getting a D or F in class?" Three-quarters of the students raised their hands. I followed up with, "Keep your hands up if you want a better grade."

One student put his hand down.

I asked, "So you *do not* want to get a better grade?"

He said, "No!" Everyone in the class laughed.

I said, "That's great news. Does your teacher know you don't want to get a better grade?" I asked the teacher, "Did you know this about this?"

She replied, "No, I didn't."

I said to her, "This is great! You can stop teaching him, because he will never give you what you want. He doesn't want to learn. This is exciting!"

I wasn't joking. I then asked him what he did want to learn. He explained he loved race cars. He wanted to be a race car driver. I asked him to find his racing heroes and learn what kind of education they had. I explained that most, if not all, will have graduated from high school or gotten a GED. He was suddenly more interested in learning.

I asked, "Does it feel good to fail?"

He said, "No."

I asked, "When you don't know the answer, do you get help?"

He said, "No."

I asked, "Why not?"

He said he didn't like to ask for help. He didn't want to feel stupid. It was scary for him. The teacher didn't realize he was so afraid to get help. It ends up this student had been rejected for so many years, he gave up. It was too dangerous for him to ask for the help. He couldn't risk getting rejected one more time. I later learned that he was a foster child who had been hurt by the adults he had trusted and asked for help. It was now safer for him to not want. Instead, he learned to hate, hide, and attack to protect himself.

Some of us never learn how to answer the question "What do I want?" We go through life doing what others want instead. We can give off the appearance of being successful and accomplished, yet we still struggle to answer this question.

I was at a private school hosting a program for high school juniors. I asked everyone to close their eyes and let go of all their fears and inhibitions. I instructed them, "Imagine a world where you could experience anything you wanted. You are guaranteed success. There is no

11

rejection. No judgment. No fear. No shame. Nothing is out of your league. You are the commissioner. You make the rules. What do you want?"

A few minutes passed. A girl raised her hand in confusion.

I asked, "What do you need?"

Frustrated, she said, "I can't do this. I don't know how to do this."

I asked, "Why?"

She said, "My parents and teachers have always told me what I should want. No one has ever asked me what I wanted. I don't know how to do this."

I got chills.

She was seventeen years old and didn't know how to want. Her parents and teachers did her wanting for her. She just followed their directions. Her parents wanted her to be the best so the best schools will want her, the best employers will pursue her, and she can have the best life. That's all well and good until someone opens her eyes twenty years later with a job she hates, a partner she doesn't want to be with, and a life that lacks joy and purpose.

What's fascinating is that you can be horrible at going after what you want and appear to have it all. It's the secret shame of being popular, attractive, and talented. It's the curse of being wanted.

I was walking back to my car with a star college quarterback following a speaking event. He had a confession to make. He struggled going after what he wanted because he was too afraid his teammates would judge him if he failed and got rejected. He only dated girls who liked him, he went to a school that wanted him, and he took on leadership positions offered to him. He was too scared to go after what he *really* wanted. He had an image to uphold. He didn't want to let the team down. While he could throw an interception, punt on fourth down, and take a loss, he couldn't see that life off the field was the same game. No one wins all the time. The game is to learn and grow. He was too afraid. For him, rejection off the field created shame. He didn't have the emotional training to take risks off the field.

According to data from the American College Health Association's National College Health Assessment, 55.9 percent of all college students reported feeling hopeless in 2019. This number was 45.2 percent in 2011. Students who have lost hope have lost the ability to want something more. We must change this.

At a recent event with Dartmouth's student government, I asked the seniors to share their greatest rejection stories and how these life lessons had helped shape them. The younger, perfectionist students watched with jaws dropped and eyes wide. They were mesmerized. One senior spoke of getting dumped by his girlfriend. Another spoke about a painful election loss. The younger students had never heard about their leaders' struggles. Everyone shares their victories on social media, but those are only quick snapshots that purposefully exclude the long, painful backstory. The discomfort is hidden from view.

Give Yourself Permission

If you want to create, change, or experience anything that's meaningful in life, you have to be vulnerable. Imagine you live in a world free of judgment, fear, shame, and failure. Anything you want is within reach. You are guaranteed success.

Want to be happier? Want to be healthier? Want to find love? Want a better job? Want to be better *at* your job? Want to help more people? Want to travel? Want a promotion? Want better grades? Want to help your children? Want an education? Want better fitting pants? Want a better relationship? Want to heal from the past? Want to do more for others? Want to do something you've always wanted but have been too afraid to do?

What do you want to create, experience, or change?

Give yourself permission to want it so badly that it would hurt if you didn't get it. Invest emotionally, or it will *not* work. Remember when I said you're guaranteed success? Success isn't defined by getting what you want every single time. It's defined by engaging in a process. Once you define what you want, you'll need to take action to get it. Prepare to face one of three possible outcomes:

1. **You will get what you want.** Getting what you want is what I want for you. When you get what you want using the process in this book, you'll understand how you got it and why you're worthy of having it. You will have a support system in place and the ability to stay empowered, energized, and excited. Getting what you want will be easier, accessible, and more consistent.

2. **You will not get what you want.** This is no longer going to be a problem for you. Not getting what you want will leave you curious and interested in finding answers. You will learn how to filter through feedback so you can get what you want or get something even better. You will no longer fear

failure, run from rejection, or define your self-worth based on being wanted.

3 **You will get what you want and lose it.** The only thing harder than not getting something is to get it, love it, and lose it. Not being able to get it back again is painful. The process in this book will help you understand how you got it, how you lost it, and how to get it again. If it's not possible (you are retired, your ex has moved on, you're dealing with medical issues), you will shift what you want and use your new skills to take other risks. You can celebrate the past, embrace the future, and find something even more meaningful to want.

> You don't need to know what you want for the rest of your life. Start with what you want for lunch. Then continue wanting.

THE PROCESS

- ☑ Want Something
- ❑ Get Comfortable with the Uncomfortable
- ❑ Think People, Places, and Patience
- ❑ Tell Your Story as If It Has Already Happened
- ❑ Celebrate, Reflect, and Repeat

EXPERIMENT 1

Identify one thing you want to create, change, or experience in the next ten months. You can change your mind at any time. The only requirement is for you to identify something. If you are too afraid to want something or don't know how to want something, you can complete this step after Chapter 2.

WARM-UP WANTS

1. What do you want for lunch today?

2. What do you want to do this weekend?

3. What's one adventure you want to go on in the coming year?

2.

Get Comfortable with the Uncomfortable

No one is more hated than he who speaks the truth.

—PLATO

If you do this right, it's going to be uncomfortable at times. Change is uncomfortable.

I used to fight change. It was a combination of fear of the unknown and stirring up pain from the past. Some changes are welcome and voluntary. Others are unwelcome and forced on us. We don't always get to choose. For example, I'm losing my hair (unwelcome).

I got married (welcome). I once rear-ended a police car (unwelcome). I found a lost set of car keys after they had been missing for two years (so welcome). I was born (welcome). I will die (unwelcome). Fighting change won't stop time from moving forward. Change is a law of nature.

If you are reading this book on earth, you are experiencing gravity. This is another law of nature. Fighting it would leave us stuck on the ground, hating everything in the sky that flies. Seasons are another law of nature. No matter what I do, it will get cold in Chicago (my home). I can choose to fight it, but then I'd just be cold *and* miserable. So I accept it. I wear several layers of clothing, a winter coat, a hat, gloves, clunky snow boots, and big wool socks (I love my warm socks). I could move to Florida, but then I'd have to deal with rain, humidity, hurricanes, flooding, tornadoes, or other forces of nature (my wife doesn't like the heat). There's no escaping the laws of nature.

Now, let me introduce you to another undeniable

law of the universe you will face when going after what you want. There is a universal truth that most people are unaware of, even though it has profoundly impacted all of us. In order to familiarize you with this law of the universe, I'd like to introduce you to Kathy. I met Kathy during a workshop for teachers and professional staff. I was extremely nervous for this event. I had never hosted a five-hour workshop for teachers on a beautiful summer day. I could see it on their faces. No one wanted to be there.

I kicked off the event by asking the attendees to share their truth with me. I wanted to know how they were *really* feeling that morning. I asked them to text me using a scale from one to ten (one = miserable, ten = happier than ever). I then asked them to text me why they were miserable or happier than ever. This way, if they looked miserable, I knew they started the morning miserable. It wasn't me. I also wanted to understand what was making them uncomfortable. The answers flooded in: sick kid, carpool, dinner plans, too much work, anxious to grade papers, remodel at home, ill parents, marital problems, not enough money, out-of-town guests coming. There were so many changes and challenges.

About forty-five minutes into the event, I asked for a volunteer to share a story about a student who was a nightmare in the classroom but later turned out to be a source of hope and inspiration. That's when Kathy volunteered to share. She had had a horribly difficult student who tormented everyone at the school. Years later, the student tracked her down to tell her how much he appreciated her unwavering kindness and love. Her story brought tears to people's eyes. Kathy cried too. She never realized how much this meant to her.

During the lunch break, I had an impromptu visit with Kathy. We talked for an hour about her life. It was like we had known each other forever. She shared what was *really* going on that day, what was behind all her emotions. She was dealing with a tremendous amount of pain. Her relationship with her stepson was making life unbearable at home. It disrupted her sleep, strained her marriage, and interfered with work. She wanted her stepson's love and respect. She felt she deserved it for all she had done for him. But all he did was push her away. The more she tried to love him, the more he fought back. The rejection was wearing her down. She was angry, hurt, and resentful. She was close to giving up. But she learned something that day.

She lit up and said, "Thank you for this." She cried tears of joy. Then she said, "Why didn't anyone tell me about this, Harlan? Why didn't anyone tell me this before? It's just so simple." She pointed to the words she had circled several times in her notebook:

THE UNIVERSAL REJECTION TRUTH

The Universal Rejection Truth

The Universal Rejection Truth says that not everyone and everything will always respond to you the way you want. Like gravity, there's no escaping this irrefutable law of nature. Like the winter in Chicago, fighting it will leave you cold and miserable.

Accepting this truth changes *everything*. It sets you free. The minute you acknowledge, accept, and embrace the Universal Rejection Truth is the moment you can surrender to the universe. This doesn't mean you give up. It means you can stop fighting and start listening when things don't go your way. There's no longer any reason to hate, hide, blame, or attack people who don't give you what you want. No one is required to give you *anything*. Let me repeat that. **No one is required to act or react one way or another.** All you can do is share what you want, listen, and see what happens next.

The Universal Rejection Truth pops up at work, at school, at home, in our personal lives, in our friendships, and in our families. No matter how much or how little you have, no matter where you come from or where you've been, not everyone and everything will always respond the way you want. Whether you're rich, poor, tall, short, young, old, male, female, both, or neither, you will encounter this truth. Without knowledge of this truth, we blame ourselves or other people when life doesn't give us what we want. We end up hating someone, something, or ourselves. Embracing the truth gives you somewhere to go. Don't hate the person who said no. Don't blame the person who didn't buy your product. Don't attack the teacher who offered you the uncomfortable truth. Process information without letting your emotions get in the way. Stop requiring people to say, do, respond, and react the way you want.

Let this sink in. **It's a law of the universe.**

The COVID-19 pandemic is a perfect example of the Universal Rejection Truth. We didn't want it and we couldn't control it. All we could do was control how we responded to it. The choice was to fight it or face it. Fighting it means blaming, hating, or hiding. Facing it means embracing the discomfort and walking alongside it. It will pass and things will get better. Embracing the truth gives us the ability to look beyond the discomfort and find hope.

Today is the day you can stop trying to control the world and embrace what is happening. There is a law of nature at play, and it's more powerful than you are. Focus on what you can control and, without judgment, give the world permission to act and react.

Once you accept the Universal Rejection Truth, you can respond instead of reacting. Reacting is emotional. Responding is activating a process that allows you to be present while taking in information in real time. You can manage what life presents you without everything having to be exactly as you want or expect it to be.

I like to live by the 90/10 rule. The 90/10 rule says that life is 90 percent amazing and 10 percent BS. In other words, if you live to be a hundred years old, that's ten years of terrible, awful, uncomfortable moments. The

discomfort can come in short spurts. It usually peaks during times of unwanted or unexpected change. If you're a real curmudgeon, you can live by the 80/20 rule. Here's the trick. When you fight the 10 percent, it multiplies. It consumes 100 percent of your time. The only way to get through the uncomfortable is to become friends with it, understand it, and allow it to walk alongside you.

This mindset has changed my life. I genuinely believe that no one is required to respond to me any other way than the way they are going to respond. My wife doesn't have to think I'm right (and yet I can still be right). People don't have to book me to speak at their events (and I still have value). My kids don't need to laugh at my jokes (but I can still be funny). If someone's response makes me uncomfortable, it's my job to figure out why I'm uncomfortable. I own it. I can't script other people. I want to learn from and understand their reactions. I can't control anyone but myself. I can try, but nature will always win.

Fact: bosses, coworkers, friends, families, strangers,

governments, drivers, animals, insects, and weather are going to be difficult at times. It doesn't matter how smart, attractive, rich, hardworking, or amazing you are—this is how the world works. Choose to fight it or face it. Fighting it will make you miserable. Facing it will change your life.

> When you require everyone and everything to respond in only one way, there's no way to be happy, because you will never get what you always want. That's nature.

The Three Types of Rejection

When I was a senior in college, I won money at the race-track. (It was a $2 bet that turned into $450, but that's a whole other story.) I decided to use the money to pay the airfare to visit my brother in California over winter break. He was working as a writer in Los Angeles at the time. I called him with the news. He was excited. He suggested that I try and get a summer internship while visiting him. This scared me. LA was far away. Plus, I was in a new relationship, and I didn't want my girlfriend to dump me. (I had a history of getting dumped.)

He then said something that totally freaked me out. It upset me. He suggested, "Why don't you try and get an internship at the Tonight Show with Jay Leno?"

I snapped back, "That's a stupid idea," and abruptly ended the conversation.

No, it wasn't a stupid idea. I was just too scared to allow myself to think about getting the internship. Who was I to get such an incredible job? I had no connections at NBC. I didn't know anyone. Plus, I struggled with feeling good enough. I felt like he was setting me up to get hurt and fail. I didn't want to put myself in that position.

After walking around the student union for thirty minutes, I started to think about what he had said. Someone needed to get the internship. Why not try? It wasn't like the odds were in my favor. What did I have to lose? I got over my self-rejection and took the risk.

I called information and got the number for NBC Studios. I asked to be connected to the person who handled internships. Within seconds, I was talking to Regina Ackerman. A month later, I was at NBC Studios, interviewing for the job. I got it. That summer, I interned at the *Tonight Show*. (And no, my girlfriend didn't dump me.)

In order to take this risk, I had to overcome something called self-rejection. I had to stop rejecting myself in order to go after what I wanted. See, I was an expert at self-rejection. There were countless women I never asked out, leadership opportunities I didn't seek, and people I never approached because I was too afraid they wouldn't give me what I wanted. But that day, I made the call. And it changed my life.

Sometimes, your risk will go as planned. Sometimes, it won't. When it doesn't go as planned, you might use the expression "it is what it is." The problem is that this doesn't really explain what "it is." Too many times, people jump to "it is what it is" because they're too

afraid to seek the truth (or they don't know how to). If you want to understand why you're not getting what you want, you will need more information to help you identify and understand the obstacles you're facing and how to get over them.

To do this, you'll need a deeper understanding of the three types of rejection that keep people from getting what they want.

1 **Self-rejection:** The act of rejecting yourself before allowing anyone else to reject you. Some people take one or two risks and stop. The process is too painful. They reject themselves before ever giving anyone else a chance. It's safer and less humiliating. It's why I almost didn't go after the internship.

EXAMPLES: You don't apply for the job. You don't ask someone out on a date. You don't ask, investigate, or try because you know it won't happen or fear getting hurt. You don't believe you are worthy or deserving. If you do get rejected the first time, you don't ask again, apply again, try again, or love again. You don't ask for help because you fear being judged, exposed, hurt, or humiliated.

② **Rejection by circumstance:** There's a reason you are not getting the results you desire. It might have something to do with you or nothing to do with you. Your job is to discover why you are not getting what you want. If you learn that the circumstance is you, then figure out if you are willing or able to change. If the circumstance is something other than you, determine if there is anything that can be done to change the outcome in your favor.

EXAMPLES: You don't get a job because you learn someone with more experience got the position. You ask someone on a date, but they reject you because they are in a relationship. You don't win the $430 billion Mega Power Money jackpot because you have the wrong numbers. You don't win the election because not enough people voted for you. Someone bought a competitor's project because it was less expensive.

3 **Raw rejection:** You will never get what you want from someone or something because of a quality or character trait. It can't be changed. You must accept raw rejection. With knowledge of the Universal Rejection Truth, this is now possible. You can still have value and not always get what you want. It's a law of nature. Remember, not everyone and everything will always give you what you want. You can have tremendous value and still face raw rejection.

EXAMPLES: You don't get the date because your ears are too big or you're too short. You are rejected because of your gender, race, or religion. You can't run for president in the United States if you are not born a U.S. citizen. Someone will not hire you because of your age.

Raw rejection can be unfair, immoral, and just plain wrong. It's systemic racism, sexism, and other -isms. Millions of people are rejected before ever taking their first breath. It's happened throughout history. If you are a woman, a minority, an immigrant, LGBTQ+, or someone who is otherwise "different," you will face more rejection, discrimination, and obstacles. You can choose to hate, hide, and attack, or you can face the Universal Rejection Truth and think people, places, and patience. Ask yourself who you want to be. Align yourself with people who have already been rejected and gotten to the places you want to go. Use their insight and experiences to inform you and guide you. Step three will help you find people and places so you can overcome the Universal Rejection Truth of being born into a culture where you may have to work harder to get where you want to go.

FAMOUS REJECTIONS

- Walt Disney was fired from the *Kansas City Star* because they said he lacked creativity.

- J. K. Rowling was a single mom who was rejected by countless publishers before her book *Harry Potter and the Philosopher's Stone* was accepted.

- Albert Einstein struggled getting his first job out of college.

- Abraham Lincoln had a nervous breakdown and lost most of his elections.

- Michael Jordan was cut from his freshman high school basketball team.

- Lady Gaga was dropped from her first music label.

- Ellen DeGeneres was ostracized after coming out as a lesbian on her network TV show.

- Steve Jobs was fired from Apple (the company he founded).

- Oprah Winfrey faced poverty, racism, sexism, and abuse.

Every hero, athlete, teacher, performer, artist, businessperson, couple, parent, veteran, mentor, and hero has faced rejection, overcome rejection, and used it to grow, learn, and help them get to places they wanted to go.

When you understand the Universal Rejection Truth, taking risks is an entirely different experience. In the past, when you took a risk without knowledge of the Universal Rejection Truth, there was a villain-or-victim mentality. If a risk didn't go as planned, someone needed to take the blame. It was time for you to hate, hide, or attack.

Now that you are aware of the Universal Rejection Truth, you are able to apply a new filter to help you process outcomes. Rejection doesn't have to be so personal. When you don't get what you want, your only job is to discover why. You need more information. Are you rejecting yourself? What is the circumstance? Is it something you can't change? Seek information.

Information is not emotional.

We make it emotional. It's simply data. Your new skill is processing the information so it informs you and helps you move forward. The danger is that the truth will make you uncomfortable. Chapter 3 will help you increase grit and become more resilient so you can tolerate the truth and allow it to inform you.

Remember Kathy?

Kathy saw the truth. She was no longer a victim, and her stepson was not the villain. The Universal Rejection Truth allowed her the freedom to seek new information. Hating, hiding, or attacking no longer served a purpose. She could stop and discover what her stepson really wanted—even if it wasn't what she wanted. Once she surrendered to the truth, she could look inward, look outward, and move forward. She could connect with her stepson from a place of love without judgment or conditions. Once she was able to be present and listen, she could process why she wasn't getting what she wanted. Was it self-rejection, rejection by circumstance, or raw rejection? And if for any reason it was raw rejection, she could still be the best and most loving mom, because the Universal Rejection Truth says not everyone and everything will always respond the way we want. Not all stepchildren will respond the way a stepmom wants. She can be loving, kind, and caring, and still not get what she wants. Hating, resenting, and blaming her stepson or herself won't change the outcome. It will just make it worse. Kathy was free to find answers without judgment and shame.

The same approach works when dealing with unwanted outcomes with family, friends, colleagues, coaches, coworkers, children, students, and strangers. Practice getting comfortable with the uncomfortable. When you want something and feel discomfort, instead of hating, hiding, or giving up, seek information.

Once you give yourself permission to get comfortable with the uncomfortable, and get in the habit

of applying this process, it will become easier to shift expectations and listen. You can empathize and validate other people's feelings without feeling threatened. The truth is no longer something to fear. It's something to discover.

Getting comfortable with the uncomfortable means looking at life through a new lens. You can say what you think and express how you feel without being attached to fixed expectations. You can take risks and go after what you want while being open to all outcomes. Results inform you. They allow you to process, learn, and grow. Risk taking becomes about learning. This is what it means to have a growth mindset.

Carol Dweck coined the term *growth mindset* in her popular book *Mindset: The New Psychology of Success*. People who have a growth mindset believe skills and intellect can change over time. We can learn and grow. Results inform us so we can gain knowledge and insight. The opposite of a growth mindset is called a *fixed mindset*. People with a fixed mindset believe that your skills, value, and intellect are fixed. There is no room for growth. This is why rejection is so painful for people with a fixed mindset. Rejection for them is a reminder of their shortcomings, flaws, and inadequacies. Embracing the Universal Rejection Truth is fundamental to having a growth mindset. It allows you to struggle, fail, get rejected, and still be brilliant.

For years, I thought I was stupid because I compared myself to other people in the classroom. I wasn't stupid. I'm just a messy learner. Freshman year in high school, I actually failed algebra. When I took it over the summer, I got an A. It took me two or three times to get it right. I later realized that I get things wrong, but then I get them right. I just need to keep trying. I learn differently. I don't lose. I win or learn. It's what smart people do.

The beauty of the Universal Rejection Truth is that it makes it safe to grow and learn. You can be amazing, intelligent, and talented...and still not always get what you want. You no longer need to feel shame when you get it wrong. You can instead feel grateful, because you know how to get the information needed to get the results you desire. If for some reason you don't get exactly what you want, you'll arrive in a place informed by life experiences that will set you on a new trajectory toward different doable dreams.

You can finally shut down your shame factory. The shame factory is the part of your brain that is always focusing on your flaws, insecurities, and failures. Instead, you can power your dream factory. The dream factory is the place where you are inspired to create, change, and experience whatever you desire. Only one factory can run at a time. Shame is boring. It's time to dream big.

When you embrace the Universal Rejection Truth, you are set up for success, because engaging in life becomes safer and more forgiving. Rejection and discomfort are part of the process. You are always learning and growing. It's a beautiful way to live.

There are no limits with this mindset. **Nothing is out of your league.** You are the commissioner who makes the rules. You are the creator of your future. Free yourself. Take comfort in knowing that rejection is not solely a reflection of your value. It's part of a natural process. It's normal. Once you fully embrace this truth, the world will change. You will stop measuring success by being wanted or liked. Instead, you will surrender to this law of nature and focus on going after what you want. Once you get comfortable with the uncomfortable, you can face all forms of rejection. You become a superhero. Nothing can stop you. Obstacles turn into opportunities. Adversity becomes a teacher. Nothing will stop you. You will either win or learn.

You can be the ripest, juiciest peach in the world, and there's still going to be somebody who hates peaches.

—DITA VON TEESE

THE PROCESS

- ☑ Want Something
- ☑ Get Comfortable with the Uncomfortable
- ❑ Think People, Places, and Patience
- ❑ Tell Your Story as If It Has Already Happened
- ❑ Celebrate, Reflect, and Repeat

EXPERIMENT 2

What do you want to create, change, or experience? (List again.) What risk excites you? What risk gives you hope? What risk can make you happier and healthier?

List three risks you can take that would make you excited for the future.

Be as specific as possible.

Examples:

1 I want to earn an associate's degree, college degree, or become specialized in a trade so I can get a better job and take care of myself and my family.

2 I want to change my eating habits and exercise four times a week so I can lose weight, get off my medication, and increase my chances of living longer.

3 I want to find love so I can build a solid relationship, get married, and have a child.

What makes you uncomfortable about taking these risks? Be very specific. List things that scare you, intimidate you, or make you anxious.

Examples:

1 I'm afraid to dream about going to college because I don't have enough money to pay for school, and no one in my family has gone to college.

2 I'm anxious to commit to changing my eating habits and exercise routine because I've gotten healthy in the past, but I gained back all the weight (and then some).

3 I'm scared to find love because I'm extremely shy, hate rejection, and don't want to get hurt.

Choose one for your risk-taking experiment. Save the rest of the risks for later.

3.

Think People, Places, and Patience

If you don't like something, change it. If you can't change it, change your attitude.

—MAYA ANGELOU

Who are your people? Where are your places? How long will it take to get where you want to go?

I went to college at the University of Wisconsin in Madison. I arrived on campus ready to experience the best years of my life. I was in a new place, surrounded by new people, experiencing new feelings. I expected my roommate to be my friend. He asked me if I wanted to get high the first week. He liked marijuana. I told him, "No thanks, man. I'm full." He moved out the following week. I tried to join a fraternity, but I didn't get in. I didn't play sports, I'm not good at male bonding, and I was bad at elaborate handshakes.

I was in love at the time (it was a miracle). My long-distance high school girlfriend was always there for me. But then we grew apart. Her father compared our relationship to a dying puppy, urging her to shoot the puppy and break up with me. She shot the puppy, and it was over. I was all alone on campus.

Everyone else seemed to be having the time of their lives, but I felt defective, depressed, and alone. I felt intense shame. I decided I would transfer. I finished the year and didn't come back. I transferred to Indiana University. I had friends at IU, and I had been visiting since I was ten years old. There was a fraternity that had to accept me (I was a legacy). The change was still hard, but I knew what to expect. I gave myself

permission to feel uncomfortable. Eventually, I found my way. I started writing for the campus newspaper, was a founding member of an improv group, and met a girl. I created a life I loved. I found my people, places, and patience.

Like a boxer who enters the ring, you'll need to train for the sport of taking risks. You'll need to tolerate the unavoidable discomfort that comes with taking risks and going after what you want. You need to be able to believe in your value regardless of the outcomes. Training means working to be your physical, emotional, and spiritual best. Training physically takes getting comfortable in your skin. Training emotionally means getting comfortable with what's between your ears. Training spiritually means working to create love and meaning in your life that isn't dependent on anyone else but you. Training is essential. It's how you develop grit and become more resilient.

For example, let's say your risk is asking someone on a date. Before taking the risk, you feel like a 9.5 out of 10. When you take your risk, you need to be able to maintain that 9.5 regardless of the outcome. It's natural to feel like a 2.5 for a few minutes should you face rejection, but training will help you build the strength, stamina, and confidence to bounce back faster and stronger. It will enable you to face the truth and continue taking risks.

Face Your Truth

I was in my early twenties living in a studio apartment (everything always happens in a studio apartment). I stood in front of the mirror in my underwear. I looked at myself for a good five minutes. I was embarrassed. I was disgusted. The feelings were raw. It was painful. I didn't love me. I didn't even like me. I *hated* me. I wanted love in my life so badly, but I couldn't expect anyone to love me if I didn't love myself. This was my uncomfortable truth: I was the problem.

I looked longer. No more excuses. I made a promise to me. I would change what I didn't love, and I would work to tolerate what I couldn't change. I'd work to be the best version of me. I'd later call this training physically, emotionally, and spiritually. This meant getting fit, accepting my feelings, and learning to love myself. I gave myself ten months to transform; I figured this was how long it takes to create a new human life (as any mom can tell you, pregnancy actually lasts forty weeks).

I wanted to do something that would change *me*. I

wanted to have a life experience that would shatter my sense of self. I lived in downtown Chicago at the time. Every year, I'd watch tens of thousands of people run by my door as part of the Chicago Marathon. I'd go outside and cheer, usually eating a muffin and drinking coffee. I'd think, "Yeah, I'd like to do that someday." Then I'd go back to sleep.

I decided I'd run the Chicago Marathon. I had never run a marathon. The most I had run was a few miles. I didn't know where to start. So I started with people. I found friends who ran marathons. I then discovered an amazing place, the Chicago Area Runners Association (CARA). The group was open to anyone at any level. It included group runs, training, and meetings. I joined. I now had my people and place.

The training started in the spring and went through October. I'd get up at the crack of dawn and run. The training was absolutely brutal. Each week, the distance increased. The longest run was eighteen miles. I had injuries. I'd sneeze uncontrollably for twenty-four hours after long runs (horrible allergies). I experienced pain, strains, and soreness. It was emotionally grueling. I could have quit several times, but I didn't. CARA helped me remain patient.

Race day came. I ran with my CARA group. My family cheered for me along the route. When I ran past my apartment, I wasn't watching—I was running. I finished the race. It changed me. There were no limits. I broke through. I haven't stopped since.

Change What You Don't Love Tolerate What You Can't Change

What is your truth? When you look in the mirror, what do you see?

I'm a white male who is five feet five and a half inches, and I weigh 162 pounds. My ears stick out. I'm forty-seven years old. I was born in the United States. I'm a writer and speaker. I graduated from Indiana University. I'm married with three children. My sense of humor is dry and sarcastic. I'm Jewish (some people will hate me for this). I can't control what anyone thinks about me. So I've stopped trying. All I can do is change what I don't love and tolerate what I can't change.

> What others think of me is none of my business.
> What you think about me is none of my business.

What I Can Change

I can change my weight, my sense of humor, my religion, and my career.

I can gain or lose weight, stop being funny, convert to a new religion, stop writing, and become a professional bowler or weatherman (two dreams).

What I Can't Change

I can't change my height, my skin color, where I was born, my ears, and my age.

I will always be a short white man from the United States who is getting older. I could get my ears surgically stitched to my head, but that would change who I am. It also might make me too good-looking. I give the world permission to not always like me or love me. I know that I'm worthy of love and have value.

When people judge me or reject me, I'm curious. I want to know why. You should be curious too. I mean, why would *anyone* not appreciate you or your ideas? If people I value in my life don't like me or my thoughts or my ideas, I want to listen and learn. Again, information is not emotional. It informs me.

Whoever you are, wherever you're from, no matter your gender, sexual orientation, race, religion, height, weight, challenges, obstacles, or upbringing, you are a beautiful person who is worthy of it all. Start by loving yourself and believing that nothing and no one can devalue you.

Look at yourself in the mirror.

Face the truth. The comfortable truth. The uncomfortable truth.

Don't hate, hide, attack, or blame.

Just face the truth. Love yourself. Change what you don't love. Tolerate what you can't change. And give the world permission to respond freely.

Finding Your People, Places, and Patience

Jackie walked into the high school cafeteria. She came back from college to offer advice to soon-to-be college freshmen. She told them, "Being poor can be great." Everyone was interested. She explained that when you tell people what you need, miracles can happen. She was a sophomore at Washington State University. She was the first person in her family to go to college. She grew up in rural Washington picking cherries and apples, harvesting onions, and working the fields since she was nine years old. She survived gang shootings, frequent moves, and challenges that would break most people. When her stepdad entered her world, life got more stable. Her parents helped her to become documented. In high school, she found GEAR UP (a federal program to increase college readiness and success). She went to college and found the College Assistance Migrant Program (CAMP), another federal program that provides support for children of migrant workers during their first year in college.

It was during her first semester that she discovered her books would cost her $400; she freaked out. She didn't have any money. She thought this might be the end. She contacted her CAMP advisor and asked for help. He said he'd see what he could do. A few hours later, he told her CAMP would buy her books for the entire year. She was beyond grateful. She learned that being poor can have its benefits. People want to help. You just need to ask.

CAMP was her place with the people who changed her life. The following semester, she considered dropping out. This time, her friend and mentor was there to help her join a sorority for professionals. Jackie is now an executive board member and leader on campus. She works in the CAMP program as a mentor. She had her "marathon moment" when she went abroad for the first time. The experience shattered her idea of just how big she could dream.

Whatever you want, whatever makes you uncomfortable, think people, places, and patience. This is how you can get wherever you want to go.

▶ **Jackie's people:** Multicultural Student Services mentor; Omar Sanchez, CAMP mentor; Evelyn Mejia, CAMP advisors; sorority sisters, parents, friends from home

▶ **Jackie's places:** CAMP program, Chicana/o Latina/o Student Center, and multicultural organizations (Greek organizations)

▶ **Jackie's patience:** Almost left school, felt self-doubt, dealt with impostor syndrome, took her a good year to find her people and places

Five Big Questions to Ask People Living the Life You Want to Live

1. Where are the three places you learned the most?

2. Who are the three people who taught you the most?

3. What was your most uncomfortable experience, and how did you get through it?

4. What advice do you have for someone in my position?

5. Can I stay in touch with you if I have questions in the future?

Who Are Your Five People?

Who are your heroes? Who do you want to become? Who are the people living the life you want to live? Who will you surround yourself with while going after what you want? You need people to help you get where you want to go. You need people to help you process the information you will discover while going after what you want. When you're feeling down, defeated, or beat up, these people will guide you, inspire you, and save you.

The people in your corner can be individuals in your daily life, people you follow on social media, authors, heroes, influencers, and role models. A lot of the people in my corner don't even know it (thank you Michael Singer, Tom Bilyeu, Tim Ferriss, Gary Vaynerchuk, Hal Elrod, and Kamal Ravikant). Some of the people in your corner can be living. Others can be loved ones who have passed. Their legacies and lessons live on. If you believe in God or a higher power, there is always someone to listen. Who are the five people in your corner?

There are three types of people to go to for help: people who volunteer, people who are asked or enlisted, and people who are paid.

Find people who will tell you what you *need* to

hear, not just what you *want* to hear. Seek out people you respect. Connect with people who have a love for teaching. Find people who know how to win. Look for people who have been there and done it. Find people who have faced it, learned from it, and won.

People Who Volunteer

These people want to help. It's rewarding for them. You are doing them a favor by allowing them to help you. Find mentors, coaches, teachers, friends, family, and people who have self-identified as volunteers. These people are safe. They are the opposite of rejection. They are welcoming. Allow them to help you.

Note: You will need to find different people to help you navigate different risks. For example, if you want to start a business, find people who have started businesses. If you want to publish a book, find people who have published books.

People Who Are Asked or Enlisted

These people can't help you until you let them know you need help. You will be surprised by their reactions. Find people who look like you. Find people from places like you. Find people who have been down the path you want to walk.

Warning: The Universal Rejection Truth says not everyone will help you. If someone doesn't respond the way you want, in the words of Taylor Swift, "Shake it off."

Many first-generation students are afraid to ask for help. They think they will look stupid or unworthy if they reveal they don't have answers. They feel like impostors. They fail to see that asking for help isn't a sign of weakness. It's a sign of strength.

People Who Are Paid

I pay a therapist to listen to me. I talk. He listens. I vomit all the thoughts on him. He cleans up the mess. Find people who are professionally trained to help.

Turn to coaches, doctors, specialists, professionals, teachers, and mentors who can help you find answers. Find authors, experts, and influencers. Look for industry leaders. Follow them on social media. Investigate their products and services. If you can't pay, ask about sliding fee schedules, scholarships, or discounts.

RANDOM ACTS OF KINDNESS

Recently, I was having dinner with a vice president of student affairs. He was talking to a member of his team about a student who had just moved into a residence hall. He explained that this student used to walk over two hours each way to school in the scorching Florida summer heat to work as an orientation leader. They had an open room and gave it to him free of charge. He didn't ask for it. They just wanted to help.

Where Are Your Three Places?

Places are where you sweat, play, pray, live, learn, lead, and love. Places are where you find friends, connection, and community. They're where you find answers and support. Finding places is how you find people when you don't know anyone. When you don't have a place, you feel lost. That's when people panic. There are always places for you to find answers and get the help you need.

Make sure some of these places are open access, meaning you don't have to be a member or be invited. These places can be virtual or physical. When you have a question or concern, go to the places to find people with answers. Let me break this down for you.

> ▶ **SWEAT: Sweat in places with people who share similar interests. Make new friends, get in shape, and build friendships while doing things that don't involve a lot of conversation. Sweating creates an instant bond.**

▶ **PLAY:** Seek out experiences that fill you with joy and happiness. If you want to experience adventure, excitement, culture, arts, competition, hobbies, or anything that makes your light shine, find places where people play. And go. Be part of a group.

▶ **PRAY:** Find spiritual groups and organizations that are open, accessible, and safe places to meet people. I tell college students, "Find a spiritual group. You don't have to be into God. You'll just meet nice people and get free food." It will work for you too.

▶ **LIVE:** Make home a place where you will be surrounded by opportunities, experiences, and energy that inspires you. Get involved in community organizations and activities that will connect you with like-minded people.

▶ **LEARN:** Use learning as a way to build connection. Schools, institutions, professional groups, and places where learning takes place give you access to teachers, experts, mentors, and peers.

► **LEAD:** Take on leadership roles that force you to be in places around other people who share common interests. Surround yourself with people who lead, and let them mentor, help, and support you.

► **LOVE:** Do things you love in places with people who share the same interests. Interact, engage, and immerse yourself in things you love. Do it face-to-face and online. Surround yourself with people who share your passion.

The Power of People and Places

Find someone you respect, admire, and want to be. Ask this person about who helped them when they wanted to give up. Ask them about the places where they found love and support when they felt the most discouraged, alone, and uncomfortable. You will *always* find people and places.

FAMOUS MENTORS

▶ **Socrates mentored Plato.**

▶ **Plato mentored Aristotle.**

▶ **Mahatma Gandhi mentored Nelson Mandela.**

▶ **Michelle Robinson mentored Barack Obama.**

▶ **Professor Dumbledore mentored Harry Potter.**

Patience: Give It Time

Patience is the ability to tolerate the discomfort you will experience while going after what you want and know it will pass. This will take time. You need to give yourself time to find the people and places to help you get where you want to go.

I met a nursing student who had failed organic chemistry three times. She finally passed on her fourth try. She didn't feel good about herself. Failing three times can do that to someone. She went to her doctor for a checkup. He asked about her studies. She shared her embarrassing story about failing organic chemistry. He confided in her that it took him five tries to pass.

Stop comparing yourself to anyone but who you were yesterday. I stopped doing this. I used to look at other people's treadmill screens at the gym. I'd see if I was running faster or longer. Then I realized this was absurd. As far as I know, the person next to me was told he would never walk again, yet he's running. All I know is what I know about me. We all run at different paces. But we can all get to the same place.

Google the word *patience* and you will get four billion results in 0.4 seconds. We expect answers in milliseconds. We shout to Alexa, Siri, and Google, and we

get answers on the spot. We don't want our texts to be left on Read. We aren't good at waiting.

Patience is the hardest part of this process. It gives you time to think. It forces you to be with yourself. Our minds take us on wild adventures. We start to question our self-worth. We tell false narratives. We second-guess ourselves. Doubt creeps in. We question things that don't need to be questioned. We have conversations that don't need to be had. We become paranoid. This is why you must practice patience while leaning on your people and finding your places.

When you get impatient, turn to your people. Ask them how long it took for them to get what they wanted. Ask them to share their most uncomfortable experience and how they got through it. Find podcasts, blogs, and books. Listen to people's stories, and you will realize your heroes almost gave up but persevered and won. And practice mindfulness. Research tells us that simply calming the mind can improve your life, health, and well-being.

Remember everything is changing. Jobs are invented. People get fired, get hired, retire, and die. Positions will open. Trends come and go. Bell-bottoms will come back in style.

It took me nine years to become a syndicated advice columnist, five years for my book to hit the *New York Times* bestseller list, and twenty years to get this book published. I haven't even listed all the things that didn't go according to plan. I've dealt with financial distress, emotional turmoil, and recently a pandemic that upended my world. When life gets hard, when I run out of answers, when I need inspiration, the answer has always been people, places, and patience. Every time I get hurt, disappointed, humiliated, or scared, I have learned from the experience. Pain is the ultimate teacher if you allow yourself to feel it (check out work by David Goggins). Be patient and trust it will be okay. Because it will.

Three Books That Will Help You Learn to Be More Patient

1. *The Untethered Soul: The Journey Beyond Yourself* by Michael Singer

2. *10% Happier: How I Tamed the Voice in My Head, Reduced Stress Without Losing My Edge, and Found Self-Help That Actually Works* by Dan Harris

3. *Love Yourself Like Your Life Depends on It* by Kamal Ravikant

Attention Teachers, Leaders, and Mentors: You are the people in the corners. You make it safe for others to share their thoughts and ideas, get comfortable with the uncomfortable, and find people in places living the life they want to live. You allow them to be patient while telling their stories and working through all the possible outcomes when they take risks. You are a gift.

WHY FIVE PEOPLE? You always have someone in your corner when you need answers. You can get a range of feedback and opinions from people you trust and respect. You can also express yourself freely knowing you will never be alone.

WHY THREE PLACES? When you have three places in your life, you always have somewhere to go and can always find something to do. If one place isn't comfortable, you always have another place to go. And we all need places.

WHY PATIENCE? Without it, you'll panic. People who panic hate, hide, and attack. When you're patient, you can think people, places, and patience.

THE PROCESS

- ☑ Want Something
- ☑ Get Comfortable with the Uncomfortable
- ☑ Think People, Places, and Patience
- ☐ Tell Your Story as If It Has Already Happened
- ☐ Celebrate, Reflect, and Repeat

EXPERIMENT 3

What makes you uncomfortable about the risk you want to take? What are the potential obstacles you may encounter? List them all.

Who are the three people who can help you overcome these obstacles? Reach out to them.

Where are the places you can find answers to help you overcome these potential obstacles? Locate these places and reach out to people who can help you.

How long will it take to get where you want to go? Ask the people in the places how long they think it will take for you to get what you want.

Note: Be open to all feedback. Info is not emotional. It informs you. Give people permission to share uncomfortable truths. Find people who want you to be successful. Talk to people who have experience addressing the obstacles you will soon face.

4.

Tell Your Story as If It Has Already Happened

"If you want a quality, act as if you already have it."
—WILLIAM JAMES

A parent came running up to me after a recent event. She was desperate to vent. Her daughter was graduating from high school the next week. Her mom thought it was a miracle she graduated because she couldn't stay focused, made poor choices, and got busted drinking. Mom had been disappointed again and again. Now, her daughter was going to college, and this parent was certain she'd fail out and end up back home. Mom wondered why she was even going to try college. But her daughter insisted on going. When this woman was finished talking, a dark cloud hovered over her.

I asked, "Do I have permission to tell you the truth?"

I ask this question when I want to be brutally honest. When I ask someone for permission, it makes it safe to share the uncomfortable truth. It's called tough love. If I tell them the uncomfortable truth without getting permission, it's called being an a-hole. This simple question gives the person responding all the power.

She let down her guard. "Sure."

I asked, "Why are you telling *this* story?"

She looked confused.

"There are two stories you can tell. One is how everything will go wrong. The other is that your daughter will figure out how to make this work. Why not tell the story where she figures it out? I know this opens you up to getting hurt and disappointed again, but you're not in her corner. You're rooting against her.

Why not root for her and give her time and permission to struggle while finding her way?"

We have the power to tell whatever story we want to tell. Some of us are experts at telling the story of the victim and the villain. It's become habit. Better to not get our hopes up. Dream small, and don't fall as far. Blame someone else. Keep the bar low, and avoid getting hurt. It works. But eventually, it leaves you empty, envious, scared, and stuck.

When you find yourself telling a story of doom and gloom, *stop*. Use your people and places to change your story. Find heroes who have been there and done it. Put yourself in places with people who found the strength and courage to create change. Learn how they told their stories. Read their books. Follow them online. Connect with them via social media. Find them in real life. We all need heroes. Soak up their stories so you know how to tell yours.

When I talk to first-generation high school and college students, I urge them to find their heroes. Find the senior you want to be. Find the professional you want to be. Find the teacher, coach, or mentor. That is you in the future. Let their stories inspire yours.

I love sharing people's stories. In *The Naked Roommate: And 107 Other Issues You Might Run Into in College,* I share stories from hundreds of students who have faced the uncomfortable, found answers, and won. The book is incredibly popular because it gives readers permission to embrace discomfort as part of the journey. It's a celebration of the good, the bad, and the unexpected. It clears the way for students to dream big.

Close your eyes, and see what you want to change, experience, or create as if it has already happened. The already happened part is essential. Trick your brain into believing it's happened. It doesn't know the difference. Allow yourself to feel it all. Be specific. Feel it. Smell it. Taste it. Touch it. Hear it. Immerse yourself in the experience of it. Be in the place where it happens. Once you feel it, open your eyes, and figure out how you got there. Instead of starting with everything you need to do and why it won't work, look back and create the story of how you were able to make it happen.

> **Leapfrog the fear, avoid the doubt, ignore the anxiety, and write the happy ending.**

How to Create Your Story

1. Identify what you want to create, experience, or change. Be specific.

2. Identify what makes you uncomfortable about what you want. Make a list.

3. Turn to your people to find answers.

4. Identify places where you can find answers.

5. Put together a timeline that allows time to learn.

Fill in the Blank:

It's _____ (fill in the date). I reached my goal and accomplished _____ (fill in the blank). The most uncomfortable part of taking my risk was _____ (fill in the blank). I was able to find answers and overcome obstacles by leaning on the following three people:

_____ (Person 1),

_____ (Person 2), and

_____ (Person 3).

I was able to find connection, community, and answers in the following three places:

_____ (Place 1),

_____ (Place 2), and

_____ (Place 3).

It took me _____ (fill in amount of time) to get here. I'm so proud of myself and my accomplishments.

Storytelling Tips

Be as detailed as possible. Use the names and titles of people who helped you. List specific places where you found information. Create exact dates and specific experiences you want to experience. Do *not* make your result dependent on other people's actions or reactions. Make it about what *you* will do. For example, don't require anyone to act or react one way or another. Make your story focused on what you will do. The rest is up to nature. Use your senses to create a colorful, vivid picture. See it, hear it, smell it, touch it, and taste it. Allow your brain to go to that place. See the people who helped you. Identify the places you put yourself to create, change, or experience what you want. Feel time pass. Experiment with different risks and different timelines.

Tell the story of your day first thing in the morning. Tell it before you go to sleep at night. Tell the story of the entire month. Tell the story of the life events that make you uncomfortable, and jump to the results you desire. Give yourself permission to feel the best-case

scenario. If telling your story as if it's already happened is too hard for you, start with a short timeline. Tell the story of your day. Then tell the story of your month. Then tell the story of your year. Then tell the story of the next five or ten years.

Story hack: *Do not* tell the story of the victim and villain. Instead, tell the story of the hero who overcame obstacles and won. You are the hero in this story.

EXAMPLES

Examples of telling your story as if it has already happened:

▶ **Change your physical appearance:** It's May 1 and I had an incredible year of transformation. I reduced my body mass index (BMI) by 10 percent. I work out four times a week for forty-five minutes, and I've improved my diet. The hardest part was changing my habits and dealing with the emotional struggles. I was able to get through it by leaning on my doctor, a fitness teacher, and an Instagram influencer. I found connection, community, and calm by attending a group fitness class, reading books on self-love in a book club, and joining Overeaters Anonymous. It took me six months to change my body. I'm so proud of myself and my accomplishments.

▶ **Change your relationship status:** I had the most incredible year looking for love. I committed to going on dates for an entire year. The hardest part was going on all the bad dates with liars and losers. I reached my goal by leaning on a dating coach, a dating author, and my positive single friends. I met new people by playing on a beach volleyball team, going on a singles volunteer mission, and giving people access to me through an online dating profile. It took me a year to find love. I'm so grateful and proud of myself.

Warning: Surround yourself with people who know how to tell stories of hope, happiness, and success. Put yourself in positive places with positive people. This process will not work if you hang out with negative people who are always numbing out, putting you and other people down, and playing the victim/villain game.

Times When I Tell My Story

1 Before a speaking event, I tell the story of the event as if it has just ended. I say to myself, "This was one of your best events. You connected with the audience on the deepest level. You were fully present. You helped and made a difference in their lives. I'm so proud of you, Harlan."

2 When I wake up in the morning and shower, I tell the story of my day. I imagine it's the end of the night, and I go through what a productive, exciting, and rewarding day it was. I go into as many details as possible.

3 When I started writing this book, I told the story of how the words flowed and poured onto the page. I journaled every single day about how joyful this process was and how it helped so many people. I hadn't written a word, but this was the story I told.

You can use this storytelling process in school, in business, and in life. If you want help telling your story, ask people you admire to share their stories. Seek out the people and places that influenced them. Ask them how long it took to get there. Give yourself permission to feel uncomfortable. Use all this to paint the picture you want to see. Release yourself from the fear and anxiety, and write about where you're going.

THE PROCESS

- ☑ Want Something
- ☑ Get Comfortable with the Uncomfortable
- ☑ Think People, Places, and Patience
- ☑ Tell Your Story as If It Has Already Happened…
- ☐ Celebrate, Reflect, and Repeat

EXPERIMENT 4

What's your story? Give yourself permission to dream it, believe it, and experience it before it happens. Imagine what it feels like to get where you want to go. Let your brain experience it with all of your senses. Give yourself permission to experience it before it actually happens. And if for any reason you get hurt or disappointed, you will have people and places to help you work through the outcome and take another risk in the future.

Now, tell your story.

5.

Celebrate, Reflect, and Repeat

> I never lose. I either win or I learn.
>
> —NELSON MANDELA

My friend Ben had a crush on his friend Emily when they were in college. Ben wanted to be more than friends. He was reluctant to share his secret. When he finally asked Emily on a date, she said no. He asked her why. She didn't see him that way. He was in the friend zone. Ben didn't blame Emily. He was prepared for all possible outcomes. Emily wasn't required to like him.

His only job was to offer an invitation to her. She didn't need to RSVP yes. When she told Ben no, he didn't hate her or avoid her or blame her. He was relieved that she knew how he felt. He was prepared for all possible outcomes. He didn't make things weird. He was comfortable with just being friends. Over time, Emily dated other guys. Ben dated other girls. A couple of years later, Emily started thinking about Ben differently. Because he had shared his feelings years earlier, she saw him differently. She wondered if he still had feelings for her. She asked. Yes, he did. They've now been married for fifteen years and have three children. This is how it works when you offer what you want without conditions, prepare for any outcome, and live in a world where you always have options.

Once you take your risk, it's time to celebrate, reflect, and repeat. Success is not about getting what you want every time. Success in this experiment is taking action without requiring anyone or anything to give you what you want. Your only job is to offer what you want to the world, listen, and learn from the information you discover.

> **Information is not emotional. It simply informs you.**

Celebrate

When I was twenty-one years old, I decided I wanted to start writing an advice column. I got the idea while interning at the *Tonight Show with Jay Leno*. That's where I met a writer who wrote advice. He gave me the idea. I went back to college and launched the column. It took off.

When it was time for me to graduate, I decided I wanted to become a syndicated advice columnist. The chances of becoming syndicated were about as good as me putting down a muffin and running a marathon. I really enjoyed that muffin.

I returned to the *Indiana Daily Student* (one of my places) and turned to my journalism teacher and newspaper advisor for help (two of my people). They showed me how to put together media kits with sample materials to submit to the syndicates. I dropped them in the mail and waited for the responses.

A couple of months passed. I received six rejections from seven syndicates. One never responded. All the rejection letters included the names of the people who didn't want me. These were my new contacts. I didn't get upset. I got to work.

I celebrated that I had information to use. I celebrated that I took a risk and people I respected reviewed my work. I celebrated that I had the confidence and courage to take action and discover the truth.

Do something and something will happen. Celebrate the act of doing something.

Reflect

I wanted to understand why I was rejected. Was it me? Was it a circumstance beyond me? Was it raw rejection?

I called the phone number on the letterhead and asked for the editorial director.

I asked, "Hi, may I please speak to Robert Levy?"

The receptionist answered, "One moment."

A new voice answered, "Robert Levy."

"Hi, Mr. Levy. My name is Harlan Cohen, and I submitted my Help Me, Harlan column to you. May I ask you a question about the submission?"

"How can I help you, Harlan?" he kindly responded.

"Thank you for reviewing my submission. I wanted to know if the column was up to your editorial standards. I also wanted to know if there is anything I can do to be part of your syndicate."

The editors were surprisingly kind. They explained that the newspaper industry was in a difficult place. Papers were cutting columns. The content was solid, but I would need to write my column for a few more years. I also needed to generate more revenue.

> *Beware:* When something doesn't go your way and you want to attack, stop. Breathe. Turn to your people. Go to your places. Give it time. Seek information. Process the uncomfortable truth. (Unless you are in immediate danger.)

Repeat

I made the changes. I got into more newspapers. I showed them the column could work. I generated more revenue. I submitted my column again. I got rejected again. This went on for nine years. Eventually, I formed relationships with several editors. Then, the legendary Ann Landers passed away. Her column was in over one thousand newspapers. Because of my relationships with the syndicates, I was offered a contract by two of them. I rejected one. I signed the other contract, and I was officially syndicated by King Features Syndicate, the largest newspaper syndicate in the world.

Your Turn to Celebrate

Success isn't about getting what you want in this experiment. Success is about sharing what you want and expressing how you feel. It's taking action and engaging in the process. It's putting whatever you want out into the world and listening. Even if you don't get what you want, celebrate. Just because you don't get the results you want today doesn't mean that won't change. The more you engage in this process, the easier it will be to get the results you desire.

Expect to get hurt at times. When it hurts, turn to your people and put yourself in places where you can find support. There will be times when you don't want to celebrate. You will want to hate, hide, and attack. You might want to give up. The moment you feel this pull, think people, places, and patience. Turn to the people you trust. Put yourself in places where you can find connection and community. Be patient. Celebrate the act of doing. Celebrate feeling your emotions. Celebrate being present. Celebrate the experience of engaging in life to the fullest and allowing the world to act and react freely.

How to Reflect

Reflecting is observing and processing feedback. It's not emotional. It's seeking information. It's facing the truth nature is revealing to you. Information will help you move forward. Yes, it might trigger certain feelings, but you are in charge of you how you process the information. You've trained for this. Your job is to understand what happened and how to use this information to move forward with confidence and clarity.

Ask these questions when you reflect:

1 Did I get what I want?

2 If the answer is yes, how did you get it?

3 If the answer is no, figure out why you didn't get it. Is the problem me? Is it something beyond me? Is it

raw rejection? If someone doesn't tell you why you got rejected, **do not assume it's you**. Assume it has something to do with them, and let the Universal Rejection Truth shoulder the blame.

Now Repeat

If you get what you want, great! If you don't get what you want, great! Use the information you'll receive, and change what you don't love or tolerate what you can't change. Turn to your people for help. Find places to get answers. If you realize you are no longer interested in taking the same risk, find a new risk.

The only way to get great at something is to allow yourself not to be great. I call this being an imperfectionist. The more you repeat the process, the better you'll become. It doesn't always take ten thousand hours to be your best. It just takes engaging in this process.

Every once in a while, a speaking event will not go

as planned. It's absolutely painful. I hate it. It cuts me to the core. When it happens, it's a punch to the gut. I can't celebrate when I'm in pain. I feel sick. My perception of my value plummets. So I reach out to my people. I call my wife. I talk to my parents. I reach out to my brothers. I talk to other speakers. I share the story and reflect. They help me celebrate that I have the courage to try and make a difference in people's lives. I listen. I calm down. Then I reflect. My self-worth jumps back up. I ask myself what I can do better. I analyze the information. The uncomfortable speaking events have made me a better speaker. I've changed over the years because of these moments. I've improved my content, changed my presentation style, and experienced incredible results.

Go after what you want. Create, change, and experience it all. You are deserving and worthy of whatever it is you want. Celebrate your risk. Celebrate the moment. Celebrate life.

THE PROCESS

- ☑ Want Something
- ☑ Get Comfortable with the Uncomfortable
- ☑ Think People, Places, and Patience
- ☑ Tell Your Story as If It Has Already Happened
- ☑ Celebrate, Reflect, and Repeat

EXPERIMENT 5

Take your risk. Celebrate whatever happens next. Process the information. If you got what you want, understand how you got it. If you didn't get what you want, figure out what went wrong. Was it you? Was it something beyond you? Can you change the outcome or not? How can you use this information to move forward? What will change should you decide to take the risk again? Repeat this process again and again. Over time, you will either get what you want or change how you go after what you want. Whatever happens, you will never lose. You will only win or learn.

"You must do the THING you
THINK you cannot do."

—ELEANOR ROOSEVELT

Conclusion

What if you lived in a world where you could go after what you wanted without fear of rejection or failure? What if you had a filter to process all outcomes and minimize the shame and discomfort? What if you no longer felt the need to hate, hide, or attack when you faced rejection or disappointment? What if you automatically thought people, places, and patience? What if you knew you would be okay no matter what?

How would your life change?

This is the framework. This is the process. Use it. Apply it. Practice it. Make it part of your daily routine.

Make it part of your life. **Give yourself permission to dream it, believe it, and make it happen.**

1 **What do you want to create, change, or experience?** Pick something small if you're afraid of reaching too high, but choose something that matters. Give yourself permission to want something that will hurt if you don't get it. This means it matters.

2 **Get comfortable with the uncomfortable.** There is a force of nature bigger than you at play. The Universal Rejection Truth doesn't discriminate. Give the world permission to not always give you want you want, but believe you can get it. Embrace and expect discomfort. Remind yourself that you are worthy of anything you want. Seek information to guide you.

3 **Think people, places, and patience.** Use your people and places to guide you, support you, and

help you. Turn to the people in your corner along the way. Put yourself in places where you can work to be the best version of yourself. Be patient and give yourself time to train, grow, and learn.

④ **Tell your story as if it has already happened.** Jump to the future. See it, smell it, touch it, taste it, and feel it. Tell your story, and believe it. Learn from people with similar stories. Surround yourself with people you want to become. Share your story, and then make it come true.

⑤ **Celebrate, reflect, and repeat.** Once you take your risk, celebrate taking action. Process the information without making it emotional. Figure out why and how you got your results. Take the same risk or take a new one. Repeat, repeat, repeat.

It's time to experience your magic.

You have everything you need. Your job is simple.

Want something. Know that you are enough. Dream it. Believe it. Make it happen.

I'm grateful to be in your corner. Let me know how I can help. Find me on social media @HarlanCohen. Find me online: HarlanCohen.com. Find me on Facebook: www.facebook.com/HelpMeHarlan.

SUGGESTED READING

▶ *Love Yourself Like Your Life Depends on It* by Kamal Ravikant

▶ *The Untethered Soul: The Journey Beyond Yourself* by Michael Singer

▶ *10% Happier: How I Tamed the Voice in My Head, Reduced Stress Without Losing My Edge, and Found Self-Help That Actually Works* by Dan Harris

▶ *Meditation for Fidgety Skeptics* by Dan Harris, Jeff Warren, and Carlye Adler

▶ *Mindset: The New Psychology of Success* by Carol Dweck

▶ *How to Win Friends and Influence People* by Dale Carnegie

▶ *Can't Hurt Me: Master Your Mind and Defy the Odds* by David Goggins

▶ *The Power of Now: A Guide to Spiritual Enlightenment* by Eckhart Tolle

▶ *The Success Principles: How to Get from Where You Are to Where You Want to Be* by Jack Canfield

▶ *Where You Go Is Not Who You'll Be: An Antidote to the College Admissions Mania* by Frank Bruni

HOW TO FIND HARLAN:

▶ www.HarlanCohen.com

▶ Facebook.com/HelpMeHarlan

▶ Twitter.com/HarlanCohen

▶ Instagram/HarlanCohen

▶ TikTok/HarlanCohen

▶ YouTube: BeforeCollegeTV

▶ LinkedIn: www.linkedin.com/in/harlancohen

▶ Email: harlan@harlancohen.com

BOOKS BY HARLAN COHEN:

▶ *The Naked Roommate: And 107 Other Issues You Might Run Into In College*

▶ *The Naked Roommate: For Parents Only*

▶ *The Naked Roommate's First Year Survival Workbook*

▶ *Dad's Expecting Too: Expectant Fathers, Expectant Mothers, New Dads and New Moms Share Advice, Tips and Stories about All the Surprises, Questions and Joys Ahead…*

▶ *Getting Naked: Five Steps to Finding the Love of Your Life (While Fully Clothed and Totally Sober)*

Message to Educators, Parents, and Business Leaders

To Educators

You are the heroes. You help our children grow to love learning. You are the people in the places who enable students to dream, believe, and make whatever they want happen. Thank you! The process in this book can be taught as early as kindergarten. It can be reinforced as students navigate the normal and natural changes and transitions (the transition to middle school, high school, and college). Too many students learn how *not* to dream. They are experts at underdreaming (the act of dreaming just big enough to not get hurt). They lose the ability to want and dream as early as elementary and middle school. We can change this.

This book will help your students adopt a growth mindset while getting comfortable with the uncomfortable. It will change how your students look at changes and challenges. When students face discomfort, instead of thinking hate, hide, and attack, you can teach them to think people, places, and patience. You can make it even safer for them to share how they feel, go after what they want, and embrace winning or learning. In addition to helping your students, use this book to embark on your own risk-taking experiment to help yourself create a life you love inside and outside the classroom.

For more exercises and activities (including a risk-taking in-class experiment), visit me at HarlanCohen .com/WinOrLearn. I'm grateful to be in your corner!

To Parents

I'm one of you. I have three kids. As someone who has been working with students, teachers, administrators, and college processionals for over twenty-five years, I've seen our kids become increasingly fragile. Teachers and administrators see it. You might see it. The data confirms it. **Our kids hate conflict, crumble when faced with rejection, and will do whatever it takes to avoid discomfort.**

They don't learn how to get comfortable with uncomfortable. They don't get a lot of practice. As a result, most students lack the life skills needed to navigate life beyond school. This book will help your child to build grit and increase resilience. It will help them get great at wanting, taking risks, and handling whatever comes next. The process works for people of all ages. It works for parents too. It's what I use to set goals, take risks, and navigate life. I'm grateful to be in your corner. Please let me know if you have questions along the way. Reach out to me on social media @HarlanCohen or via email at harlan@helpmeharlan.com.

To Business Leaders

From the new employee who fears making cold calls, to the manager who must tell an employee the uncomfortable truth, facing rejection is part of doing business. The framework and lessons in this book can be incorporated into your training and company culture. New team members will be able to express what they want and share how they feel without fear of failure, rejection, or judgment. Leaders will be better equipped to help team members set goals, overcome obstacles, and exceed expectations. Information will not be emotional. It will be data that helps your team embrace the truth and adopt a win or learn mindset. By creating a safe environment that embraces the truth, leaders will create a community built on trust, collaboration, and meaningful connection.

For information about workshops and leadership events, visit HarlanCohen.com/speaking and HarlanCohen.com/WinOrLearn.

Acknowledgments

Thank you to everyone who has rejected me. Thank you to everyone who has loved me, appreciated me, and included me. I'm grateful for all of you. Thank you to my wife, Stephanie, and my kids, Eva Kaye, Harrison, and Asher. You are my people. You are my place. You are my rock. I love being in quarantine with you. Words can't even begin to express my love for you. Thank you to my parents, Eugene and Shirlee. You are my heroes. You have always created a place where I have felt love, support, and acceptance. You have always been in my corner. Thank you to my brothers, Victor and Michael. As the youngest, you loved me, rejected me (kicked me out of your rooms), and embraced me. Thank you for always being my closest, most trusted friends. Thank you to Irene, Dan, Rozi, Marvin, and Fran—you came into my life and have always been so loving, supportive, kind, and caring. I'm so blessed and grateful for you. To my nephews and nieces, Skyler, Rae, Henry, Ethan, Hannah, and Matty, thanks for always loving me. To Dominique, Todd, Chris, Meg, MJ, Kate, Anna, Liz, and the entire team at Sourcebooks, you are a bright light and a dream partner who changes lives. I'm so grateful to have you in my corner for over fifteen years. Thank you to Eliot Ephraim for being there from the start. You always believed in me, even when I struggled to believe. A big thanks to Travis Marsala and Andy Antao. You are amazing teammates. Thank you to the late Dave Adams, Indiana University, and the *Indiana Daily Student*. Thanks for being in so many people's corners. Thank you to King Features Syndicate and all the newspapers who have picked up my column and dropped it. I am forever grateful. Thank you to all the educators, students, and professionals who have shared their wisdom, love, time, stories, struggles, and victories with me. I'm blessed to share this moment with you. Thank you.

About the Author

Harlan Cohen has been rejected more times than most human beings. He is a *New York Times* bestselling author of seven books, a speaker who has visited over five hundred high schools and college campuses, and a nationally syndicated advice columnist. His books have sold over one million copies, and he has helped countless readers navigate change and get comfortable with the uncomfortable. Harlan's most popular book, *The Naked*

Roommate: And 107 Other Issues You Might Run Into in College, is used as a textbook in high school and college classrooms around the world.

Harlan's career started at the *Indiana Daily Student* newspaper on the campus of Indiana University in Bloomington. After a summer internship at the *Tonight Show with Jay Leno*, Harlan started writing his advice column in his college newspaper. Soon, his column was running in newspapers around the world, including the *New York Daily News*. Harlan then wrote his first book, *Campus Life Exposed: Advice from the Inside*, and began speaking on campuses across the country. Twenty-five years later, Harlan is now a leading expert on social and emotional learning, leadership, grit, resilience, college readiness, navigating change, parenting, and getting comfortable with the uncomfortable. He has appeared in *The New York Times*, *The Washington Post*, and on *The Today Show*. Harlan is a journalist who uses facts, stats, and data to drive home his message. Harlan is committed to supporting educators, teachers (K-12), professionals, and anyone who wants to create positive change.

Harlan is the founder of BeforeCollege.TV and can be found on most social media. Send him a note and he'll get back to you. If he doesn't get back to you fast enough, tell him "I thought you cared." That will shake him up. Harlan lives in the suburbs of Chicago with his wife and three young children. He is grateful you have read this entire bio.

▶ **Email:**   harlan@helpmeharlan.com

▶ **Website:**   www.HarlanCohen.com

                 www.BeforeCollege.TV

▶ **Instagram and Twitter:**

                 @HarlanCohen

▶ **Snapchat and TikTok:**

                 @helpmeharlan

▶ **Facebook:**   Facebook.com/HelpMeHarlan

▶ **Linkedin:**   www.linkedin.com/in/harlancohen

NEW! Only from Simple Truths®

IGNITE READS
spark impact in just one hour

IGNITE READS IS A NEW SERIES OF 1-HOUR READS WRITTEN BY WORLD-RENOWNED EXPERTS!

These captivating books will help you become the best version of yourself, allowing for new opportunities in your personal and professional life. Accelerate your career and expand your knowledge with these powerful books written on today's hottest ideas.

TRENDING BUSINESS AND PERSONAL GROWTH TOPICS

 Read in an hour or less

 Leading experts and authors

 Bold design and captivating content

EXCLUSIVELY AVAILABLE ON SIMPLETRUTHS.COM

Need a training framework?
Engage your team with discussion guides and PowerPoints for training events or meetings.

Want your own branded editions?
Express gratitude, appreciation, and instill positive perceptions to staff or clients by adding your organization's logo to your edition of the book.

Add a supplemental visual experience
to any meeting, training, or event.

Contact us for special corporate discounts!
(800) 900-3427 x247 or
simpletruths@sourcebooks.com

LOVED WHAT YOU READ AND WANT MORE?

Sign up today and be the FIRST to receive advance copies of Simple Truths® NEW releases written and signed by expert authors. Enjoy a complete package of supplemental materials that can help you host or lead a successful event. This high-value program will uplift you to be the best version of yourself!

— SIMPLE TRUTHS —
ELITE CLUB
ONE MONTH. ONE BOOK. ONE HOUR.

Your monthly dose of motivation, inspiration, and personal growth.

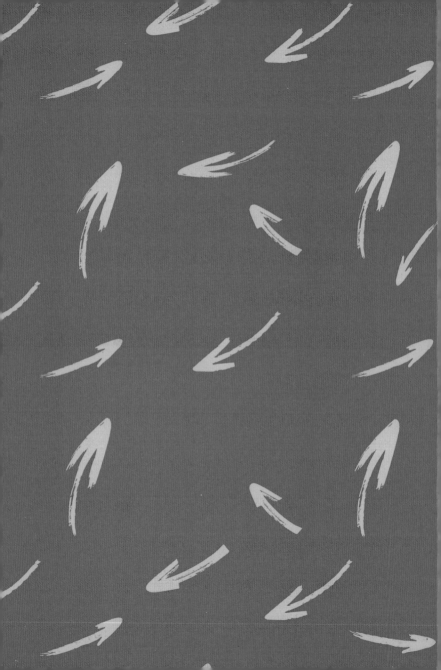